HONEST ABE'S
Guide to Presidential Elections

SEAL OF THE PRESIDENT OF THE UNITED STATES ·

By Jack Silbert

Illustrated by Jim Paillot

Scholastic Inc.

To Chad: Thanks for hanging around.
—J.S.

To Rosie, Camden, and Lisa – the legislative,
judicial, and executive branches of our family!
—J.P.

Copyright © 2012 by Scholastic Inc. All rights reserved. Published by Scholastic Inc.
SCHOLASTIC and associated logos are trademarks and/or registered trademarks of Scholastic Inc.

12 11 10 9 8 7 6 5 4 3 2 1   12 13 14 15 16 17/0

ISBN 978-0-545-48329-2

Printed in the U.S.A.   40

First printing, October 2012

Photo Credits:
Page 7: Elegant Ornate frames in black and white © LokFung/iStockphoto; Page 7: The White House in Washington, D.C., in spring with fountain and red tulips © Jeff Kinsey/Shutterstock; Page 9: U.S. Constitution © Rich Koele/iStockphoto; Page 11: New York suffragists fighting for women's right to vote hold a picket demonstration outside the White House in Washington, D.C., in Feb. 1917 © AP Photo; Page 18: 2008 Democratic National Convention © John Moore/Getty Images.

Designed by
Janet Kusmierski

CONTENTS

I was the sixteenth president of the United States. Many people consider me one of the very best U.S. presidents of all time. I was elected president in both 1860 and 1864. So I know a lot about elections!

In this book, I'm going to tell you all about presidential elections. You'll learn who can run for president, who can vote, how we choose who runs, how voting works, how the winner is decided, and everything in between. **And I'll crack some jokes along the way. I'm a pretty funny guy!**

> **Q: What do you call a dance about voting?**
>
> A: A ballot ballet!

I'm also an honest guy, so you can trust what I tell you. (Otherwise, I wouldn't have the nickname **"Honest Abe"!**)

Are you ready? Then my vote is for turning the page!

PRESENTING THE PRESIDENT

Before I talk about how we pick a president, let's learn about the job of being the president. It's a very important job. In fact, many people think that the U.S. president is the most powerful person in the whole world.

THE U.S. GOVERNMENT IS DIVIDED INTO THREE PARTS, CALLED BRANCHES.

Legislative

Executive

Judicial

The executive branch is run by the president. The president has many responsibilities.

The legislative branch is our Congress. This branch writes nationwide laws for the U.S. people.

The judicial branch is made up of courts and judges. They help explain the laws of our country, and they also decide if laws have been broken.

Why does our government have three branches? So that the different branches can check on each other, and none of them—not even the president—have total power. It's a good thing, because all that power could really go to your head. And then you'd need an even bigger hat than mine!

THE PRESIDENT'S RESPONSIBILITIES INCLUDE:

★ Approving laws written by Congress. (The president can also choose to veto, or not approve, a law from Congress.)

★ Making sure the people of the U.S. follow the approved laws.

★ Choosing people for important jobs such as judges, ambassadors, and department heads.

The president lives in the White House, in Washington, D.C. Inside the White House is the Oval Office, where the president works.

The president's family is called the "First Family." **Air Force One** is the name of the president's plane.

The other big part of the president's job is to be **commander-in-chief** of our military: the army, navy, air force, Marines, and Coast Guard. I know a lot about this part of the job—I was president during the Civil War (1861-1865), when our Northern states were fighting our Southern states!

7

The United States is a democracy, which means the citizens have a say in the decisions that affect their lives. It also means that U.S. citizens vote for the people who make many of these decisions.

These decisions are usually decided by majority: the choice of more than half of the people voting.

Let's say ten kids in your class are voting for pepperoni or mushrooms as a pizza topping. Half the number of voters is five. So, for a majority, we'd need at least six people to make the same choice. (I hope they decide soon. I'm hungry!)

The **Founding Fathers**, the people who wrote our Constitution, decided we'd have a president who would be **elected**—chosen by voters. Other countries choose their leaders in different ways. Before the United States was formed, Great Britain controlled the colonies here. Great Britain was ruled by a king. A king or queen usually rules a country for that person's whole life, and then passes on the power to a son or daughter.

The Founding Fathers thought that **kings had too much power**. So they created the three branches of government (described on pages 6–7). They also made the rules for electing the president. These rules are in the **Constitution** and its **amendments** (rules that were added to the Constitution later). According to Article II of the Constitution, the president is elected to the job for **four years** at a time. And a person can only be elected president twice. This is known as a **term limit**. So we have an election to choose the U.S. president every four years.

The U.S. Constitution was signed on September 17, 1787, in Philadelphia.

THE CONSTITUTION GIVES U.S. CITIZENS THE RIGHT TO VOTE IN PRESIDENTIAL ELECTIONS. BUT NOT EVERYONE IN THE COUNTRY IS ALLOWED TO VOTE. YOU MUST MEET CERTAIN RULES.

CITIZENSHIP

Voters must be U.S. citizens. That means a person who was born in the United States or in a U.S. territory. People who move here from other countries can also become citizens. They must fill out an application, live here for a certain number of years, learn about the country, and pass a test.

AGE

If you are reading this book, you might be too young to vote! In U.S. presidential elections, voters must be at least eighteen years old.

REGISTRATION

You can't just walk into the voting booth and say, "I'm here! I'm ready!" You must first register to vote in the state where you live. The rules, such as how long before an election you need to register, are different from state to state.

CAN'T VOTE

In almost all states, people in prison are not allowed to vote. In many states, when someone gets out of prison, he or she will be allowed to vote again.

IMPORTANT MOMENTS IN VOTING

Before, I said that U.S. citizens can vote. But not all groups of people have always had the right to vote. Here are some important changes to U.S. laws about voting:

In 1870, the **Fifteenth Amendment** was added to the U.S. Constitution. This made it against the law to stop someone from voting because of race or color.

In 1920, the **Nineteenth Amendment** to the U.S. Constitution gave women the right to vote. For more than seventy years, American women had demanded to be treated the same as men. This was an important step.

> I helped end slavery in the United States, and this amendment gave former slaves the right to vote.

American women march in front of the White House demanding voting rights.

In 1971, the **Twenty-sixth Amendment** to the Constitution lowered the minimum voting age from twenty-one to eighteen. Many people think the age should be lowered even more, to sixteen. So maybe you will get to vote sooner than you think!

11

(POLITICAL) PARTY TIME!

WHAT'S A POLITICAL PARTY? Well, you don't have to bring a present and there won't be any cake.

In this country, we have two major **political parties**: the **Democrats** and the **Republicans**. People in a particular political party feel the same way about many of the topics that are important to the country. These topics include education, energy, the economy, the military, and many, many others.

People in a political party want someone from that same political party to be elected to a **government job**, also called an **office**. This can be any office: the mayor of your town, the governor of your state, senators, U.S. representatives, all the way up to the president of the United States. And there are many other government offices in between!

The basic idea is this: If someone in your political party is elected, that person will probably support rules, laws, and changes that you also support.

Q: Why were the birds and the kitten arguing?

A: Because one was a Repub-toucan and one was a Demo-cat

HISTORY

The two major political parties in the U.S. have been around for a long time. The **Democratic Party** formed in the early 1800s, while the **Republican Party** formed in the mid-1800s.

Cartoonists will often use an **elephant** to represent the Republican Party and a **donkey** to stand for the Democratic Party. These "mascots" have been used since the 1800s.

The Republican Party is often called the "GOP," which stands for **Grand Old Party**.

OTHER PARTIES

Though most U.S. politicians and voters are either Democrats or Republicans, there are many, many other political parties in the United States. Many "**third party**" candidates have won elections for local or state offices.

Politicians and voters can also decide to be independents—not a member of any party. **Independents** have held many important political offices in the United States. There have been popular independent candidates for president. One independent candidate even won: That was **George Washington**!

People from different political parties often disagree with each other. They have different ideas about the way things should be run. Even people in the same party can disagree! It's important to remember that though we have differences, we also share many beliefs. **And things work best when we work together!**

13

The United States has often been called a place where any kid can grow up to be president. That's basically true! **The Constitution** lists only three requirements to be president:

You Must...

be a natural-born citizen of the United States.

be at least thirty-five years old.

have lived in the United States for at least fourteen years.

EVEN THOUGH ALMOST ANYONE CAN BECOME PRESIDENT, MANY PRESIDENTS HAVE HAD COMMON BACKGROUNDS.

Of the first 43 people to be the U.S. president . . .
* 18 had been in the U.S. House of Representatives
* 16 had been U.S. senators
* 25 had been lawyers
* 24 had been in the U.S. military

In the past 115 years, only one president did not go to college. (That was **Harry Truman**, thirty-third president, 1945–53.)

Most presidents have been between the ages of 50 and 59 when elected. The youngest was **John F. Kennedy**, age 43 (thirty-fifth president, 1961–63). The oldest was **Ronald Reagan**, age 69 (fortieth president, 1981–89).

Of the first 43 presidents, the average height has been almost 5 feet, 11 inches. The shortest was **James Madison** (fourth president, 1809–17) at 5 feet, 4 inches. The tallest? **Me, of course!** I am 6 feet, 4 inches tall.

Q: Why did the kid think the president was twelve inches tall?

A: He heard the president was a ruler.

SHOW YOUR PRIMARY COLORS

I just told you that almost anyone can run for president. And every four years, it really seems like almost everyone *is* running for president! But before **Election Day**, the Republicans and Democrats each need to choose just one candidate.

How do they do it? By holding events called **primaries** and **caucuses** in each state. These take place from January through June of the presidential election year.

You can think of these events as little elections in each state. The voters in that state pick which **Republican** candidate and which **Democratic** candidate they want to run for president. (If the current president has only had the job for four years, that person is almost always his or her party's candidate in the next election.)

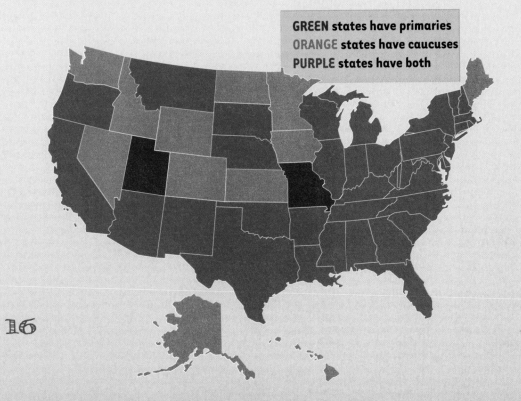

GREEN states have primaries
ORANGE states have caucuses
PURPLE states have both

PRIMARIES VS. CAUCUSES

What is the difference between these two types of events? Let's look at them.

PRIMARY

Most states hold primaries. Like most elections, primaries are done by
secret ballot. That means only you know which candidate you're voting for.
In "open" primaries, voters can choose a candidate from any political party.
For example, a Democrat could vote for a Republican candidate,
or a Republican could vote for a Democrat. In "closed" primaries,
you must choose a candidate from your own political party.

CAUCUS

A caucus is more like a series of meetings. They happen in schools, town halls,
and other gathering places across a state. Voters listen to speeches from their
party's candidates. The voters discuss their opinions. Then they
choose which candidate they think is best. It might be by a show of hands or by
breaking into groups—usually not by secret ballot.

CHOOSING DELEGATES

Primaries and caucuses are different, but they have the same purpose:
choosing which people from the state will go to a big event. These people are
called **delegates** and the event is called the political party's **national
convention**. Sound confusing? Don't worry! I'll explain it on the next page!

PAY ATTENTION TO CONVENTIONS

After all the primaries and caucuses are done, each political party holds a big event called a **national convention**. The conventions are held in a different U.S. city every four years. They take place in the late summer. The national convention is like a party for the party! But some important things happen at this party. By the end of the convention, the political party has decided who will be the one person from the party running for president. That person's choice for vice presidential candidate is also officially approved.

Here's how it works!

WHO GOES

Every state and U.S. territory sends people called delegates to the national convention. Each delegate has promised to support one of the party's presidential candidates.

ROLL CALL!

You know how in school, the teacher calls your name, and you say "Here"? They do a **roll call** at the national convention too! This is how the delegates vote. The states are called in alphabetical order. When a state is called, a spokesperson announces how many of that state's delegates are supporting each candidate.

Delegates attending a national party convention.

The winner is the candidate who gets a **majority**—remember, that's at least one more than half—of all the delegates' votes.

18

NOT A SURPRISE PARTY!

In the old days, convention voting could be very exciting. People didn't always know who the winner would be! Sometimes they would have to do the roll call over and over again. In between, delegates supporting one candidate would try to get other delegates to change their minds. This would keep happening until one candidate had a majority.

In modern times, each political party usually knows who its winner will be before the convention even begins. **How does it happen?** During the primaries and caucuses, candidates keep track of how many delegates support them. If it's not enough to win at the convention, they often drop out of the presidential race. These candidates usually tell their delegates to support the leading candidate instead. Political parties like to be united behind one candidate. So the roll-call vote is often **unanimous**—every delegate voting for the same person!

WE ACCEPT!

Finally, it's the last day of the convention. The people who have been chosen to be the party's candidates for president and vice president give their acceptance speeches. Everyone at the convention is then very happy. Delegates wave colorful signs. Balloons and confetti drop from the ceiling. Now it really looks like a party!

It's good the candidates are having fun, because the really hard work is about to begin!

CAMPAIGN GAINS

By the end of the summer in a presidential election year, we usually know who the major candidates are. There is one **Republican** candidate, one **Democratic** candidate, and sometimes a major third-party or **Independent** candidate. This is when nationwide **campaigning** really begins.

What is campaigning? It is when the candidates try to convince the American people to vote for them. The candidates explain what ideas they have and what topics are most important to them. During the primaries and caucuses, candidates campaign in each of the different states. They also try to raise MONEY from their supporters. The more money that candidates raise, the more they can campaign!

Candidates campaign by traveling from town to town, giving speeches and meeting voters. They are interviewed on TV, radio, and in news articles. Before a presidential election, you will see and hear many campaign messages and slogans. A slogan is a saying they hope you'll remember! A slogan used in my 1860 campaign was "Vote yourself a farm!" (That was because I had a plan for Western settlers to get free land.)

Vote FoR Me!

You will see campaign messages and slogans everywhere: bumper stickers on cars; signs stuck in people's front yards; posters in windows; T-shirts, buttons, and hats; websites and e-mails; pamphlets, flyers, and mailed letters; songs; telephone calls; radio commercials; and TV commercials. Lots and lots and lots of TV commercials! Candidates and their supporters spend a lot of money on TV commercials, so they can get their message to many, many viewers at the same time. Television is not only important for commercials, though. Turn the page to learn about an important time when voters tune in!

Vote FoR HoNest Abe

VoTe

vote foR LiNColN

21

GREAT DEBATES

In the month before the election, presidential debates are held. In a debate, the candidates take turns answering the same questions. The candidates for president usually have three debates. The vice presidential candidates usually have one debate. All of these debates are broadcast on television, radio, and the Internet.

THE MOST FAMOUS DEBATES EVER MAY BE THE SEVEN BETWEEN ME AND STEPHEN DOUGLAS IN 1858.

I was trying to be a U.S. senator for the state of Illinois. Douglas was already a senator, and I hoped to defeat him in the next election. People from all across the country read about our debates in newspapers.

I actually didn't win that election! However, I became much more famous because of the debates. That fame helped me win the presidency two years later! Also, my debates with Douglas led to the type of presidential debates we have today.

Of course, modern debates are a bit different from the ones held in my day. Today's debates usually have a moderator. This is the person who asks the questions that the candidates answer. Sometimes people in the audience ask questions. **The candidates take turns being asked questions.** The first candidate gets two minutes to answer. Then the other candidate (or candidates) gets one minute to speak about the same question.

Debates give people a good chance to hear the candidates' opinions on many important topics. They can really help voters make a decision before . . .

Election Day!

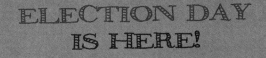

ELECTION DAY IS HERE!

Across the country, more than **one hundred million people** will vote in a presidential election. Most of these voters will go to a polling place on Election Day. Polling places are often in schools, libraries, fire stations, and other common spots. There are more than one hundred thousand polling places in the United States. Where you live determines which polling place you are supposed to go to.

At the **polling place**, there are officials who make sure the election rules are being followed. They check that people who come in are registered to vote (see pages 10–11). The voter then goes into a voting booth. This is important because the presidential election is a secret ballot. Remember: This means no one else can see or know who you voted for. **SHHH!!!!!!**

Not everyone is able to go to a polling place on Election Day. Often these are people who are sick, injured, or are traveling away from home. These people can fill in **absentee ballots** and mail them in before the election.

Absentee Ballot

After the last voter at each polling place votes, all the ballots are sent to a special location to be counted. Officials from the different political parties watch the counting to make sure it is fair. Some counting is done by computer, some by machine, and some by people.

When the counting is done in each state, it is announced which candidate got the most votes in that state. By late at night on Election Day, we usually know who the next president and vice president will be.

Even though news reports will say, "We Know Who the New President Is!" it is not official. Not yet. Turn the page to find out why!

25

Election Day is over. The candidate who got the most votes across the country is the winner, right? Well, not always, believe it or not! Why? Because the United States has something called the **Electoral College**. It's not like the colleges people go to after high school, with classes, football teams, and big buildings. The Electoral College isn't even a place! Let me explain.

Each state gets a certain number of **electors**: one for each senator (that's two per state) plus one for each U.S. representative (that number is different depending on a state's population). There are currently a total of 538 electors, who we say are "members of the Electoral College."

When you vote for president and vice president, you are not voting directly for those candidates. You are really saying, "Hey, electors for my state! You should vote for the candidate I like!"

Q: Why did the politician put on sneakers?

A: Because she was running for president!

In December, the electors cast their electoral votes. To win the presidency, a candidate needs at least 270 electoral votes. That is one more than half of the total 538 electoral votes. (Do you remember the word we use in voting when we have more than half?)

The Electoral College may sound a little strange. But our Founding Fathers had a good reason when they came up with the idea. They didn't want the smallest states, where fewer people live, to be ignored in presidential elections. **With the electoral system, every state—big or small—gets a say!**

As I said before, we usually know who the winner is on Election Day. (Newspapers and news programs unofficially keep track of the electoral votes on Election Day.) The Electoral College announces the official winner, whom we now call the president-elect. It would be very, very surprising if that was not the person we expected! However, some surprises are possible. **Turn the page to find out what they might be!**

WHAT-IFs

ELECTION DAY AND THE ELECTORAL COLLEGE USUALLY RUN PRETTY SMOOTHLY. BUT SURPRISES CAN HAPPEN!

Here is one surprise you won't see. Early in this book I said that a person could be elected president only twice. However, this didn't become the law until 1947. Before that, Franklin D. Roosevelt was elected president four times!

Now, here is a surprise that is still possible. The candidate who gets the most votes across the country (called the "**popular vote**") almost always gets the most electoral votes too. But not every time! There have been four presidential candidates who won the popular vote but not the electoral vote:

Andrew Jackson in 1824

Samuel J. Tilden in 1876

Grover Cleveland in 1888

Al Gore in 2000

Jackson and Cleveland won other presidential elections: Jackson was our seventh president (1829–37) and Cleveland was president twice, from 1885–89 and again from 1893–97.

Or let's say the vote in a state is very, very close. If this happens, states have rules to **recount** all the votes. This can take a lot of time! It famously happened in the 2000 presidential election between **George W. Bush** and **Al Gore**. The vote total in Florida was extremely close, and a recount began. It was another month and a half before we knew that Bush would be our forty-third president (2001–09)!

And what if no candidate receives **270 or more** electoral votes? It actually happened way back in 1824! Here are the rules for this: The U.S. House of Representatives then gets to choose the president. Each state in the House gets one vote, selecting from the top three presidential candidates. The House did this in 1824, picking **John Quincy Adams** (sixth president, 1825–29) over **Andrew Jackson**.

CONGRATULATIONS, INAUGURATION DAY!

Finally, it's here: Inauguration Day! This is the day when the president-elect becomes the new president! "Inaugural" is a word that means "beginning," so Inauguration Day is the beginning of a new presidential term. Here is how the president-elect spends his day.

TO THE CAPITOL!

The current president and the president-elect travel from the White House to the Capitol building together. This short two-person trip has been a tradition since 1837!

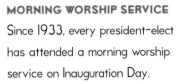

MORNING WORSHIP SERVICE

Since 1933, every president-elect has attended a morning worship service on Inauguration Day.

INAUGURAL ADDRESS

Next, the president gives a speech, called the "Inaugural Address." Every president has done this since George Washington in 1789. In the speech, the president talks about goals for the United States.

LUNCHTIME!

After the speech, the president goes inside the U.S. Capitol for the inaugural luncheon.

PRESIDENTIAL PARADE!

The president and vice president lead a parade down Pennsylvania Avenue from the Capitol to the White House. There are marching bands, floats, and a huge cheering crowd! George Washington led the first inaugural parade in 1789.

3

THE VICE PRESIDENT . . .

On the inaugural platform, the vice president-elect takes the oath of office. He or she repeats a promise to follow the rules of, and defend, the U.S. Constitution.

4

THE PRESIDENT!

At noon on Inauguration Day, the president-elect officially becomes the president. Around this time, the new president takes the presidential oath of office. The chief judge of the U.S. Supreme Court helps with this ceremony.

PARTY TIME

At night, it's time for the inaugural balls. These are big parties to celebrate the president. The first one was held in 1809.

My second inauguration was on March 4, 1865. That's a long time ago, but I remember it like it was yesterday! What a rainy, windy day it was. Still, thousands of people stood in thick mud to hear me speak. The new dome on the Capitol building was just over a year old. The Civil War was nearly over, and the country would once again be united. I was proud of our people, proud of the work we'd done, and proud to be the president.

I hope you learned a lot in this book. It will all help when you're old enough to vote for president. Or who knows? You might want to run for president! It's a good job, and you can trust me on that.

I'm Honest Abe!   31

GLOSSARY

Absentee ballot ★ If a person can't make it to a local polling place on Election Day (because of illness, injury, travel, etc.), he or she can fill out and mail in an absentee ballot before the election.

Campaigning ★ When candidates try to convince people to vote for them, through speeches, commercials, and other means.

Caucus ★ State meeting to choose a political party's presidential candidate. Many states hold primary elections instead of caucuses.

Constitution ★ The document written by our Founding Fathers in 1787 that gives the basic rules for our country and explains how our government works.

Delegates ★ People from a state who attend a political party's national convention.

Democracy ★ System of government in which the people have a say in the decisions that are made.

Electoral College ★ Our system of officially deciding who the new president is. The Election Day voting results in the fifty states decide how the electoral votes will be split up. There are currently 538 electoral votes. A candidate must receive at least 270 of these votes to become president.

Inauguration Day ★ This is the day that a new presidential term begins. There is a big ceremony in Washington, D.C., where the president and vice president take their oaths of office.

Independent ★ A voter or candidate who does not belong to any political party.

Majority ★ The choice of more than half the people making a decision, such as a vote.

National convention ★ The big meeting held by each political party to officially announce the party's candidates for president and vice president.

Political party ★ A large group of people who share many opinions about how the country should be run. In the United States, the two main political parties are the Democrats and the Republicans.

Popular vote ★ The results of all the people who voted across the U.S. on Election Day. This is different from the electoral vote. (See *Electoral College*.)

Primary ★ An election in a state between presidential candidates from the same political party. In open primaries, voters can choose a candidate from any political party. In closed primaries, you must choose a candidate from your own political party.

Term limits ★ The number of times and length of time a government official is allowed to have the same job. The president can only be elected to two four-year terms.

Unanimous ★ When everyone votes for the same person or thing.

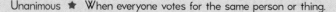